THE REFORMER

The Idealist's Guide to the Real World

Asa Eccleston Kibilski

CONTENTS

THE ARCHITECT OF CHANGE: INTRODUCING THE REFORMER ENNEAGRAM TYPE

The Reformer. The Idealist. The principled visionary with a burning desire for a better world. If you recognize yourself in these titles, you're in the right place. This book is not simply a guide to the Enneagram, but a roadmap specifically tailored for the Reformer's journey toward self-awareness and finding your place in a world that doesn't always align with your high standards.

The Essence of the Reformer

At your core, you see a world full of potential, a world that *could* be extraordinary, harmonious, and just. But the nagging sense that things are not as they *should* be fuels a restlessness within. You are propelled by the need to correct what's wrong, to leave your mark and make things better. This unwavering commitment to improvement defines the Reformer spirit.

You are the architect of change, always envisioning how systems, people, and even yourself can be refined and enhanced. You possess a keen eye for the flaws, the inconsistencies, and the imperfections that others may overlook. This gift allows you to identify areas in need of reform, but it can also lead to a hyper-focus on the negative.

The Inner Critic

Many Reformers have a powerful inner critic, constantly scrutinizing actions and behaviors. This voice, while aimed at self-improvement, can sometimes be relentless, demanding perfection that is impossible to achieve. It's important to remember that this inner critic is not the enemy but a well-intentioned, if misguided, part of your personality.

The Power of Ideals

Idealism is embedded in the Reformer's DNA. You hold yourself and the world to high expectations, sometimes impossibly high ones. These ideals serve as your compass, guiding your choices and directing your energy toward causes you deem worthy. However, it's essential to balance your idealism with a healthy dose of pragmatism, especially when those pristine ideals bump into the complexities of the real world.

The Head Center

The Enneagram teaches that we are driven by three primary centers of intelligence: the Head, the Heart, and the Body. For Reformers, the Head Center is dominant. This translates into a strong analytical mind, a love for logic, and a relentless search for meaning. Reformers analyze information, assess situations, and make decisions based on what they believe is rational and just.

This reliance on the Head Center can sometimes lead you to overthink things or make judgments that may appear rigid to others. Remember, there's much wisdom to be found in the Heart (feelings) and the Body (instincts) as well.

Embracing Your Reformer Self

This book is an invitation to delve deeper into the Reformer personality. In the chapters ahead, we'll explore your core motivations, your relationship with anger, the nuances of your wings (the neighboring Enneagram types), how your idealism colors your relationships, your strengths, and your potential shadow sides.

By understanding your unique Reformer wiring, you'll be empowered to harness your innate desire for improvement, temper your inner critic, and navigate the often messy world with wisdom and grace. Ultimately, this journey of self-discovery will help you channel your idealism into meaningful action, leaving a positive imprint on the world, one step at a time.

SEEING THE WORLD IN PERFECT HARMONY: THE REFORMER'S CORE MOTIVATION

If there's one phrase that sums up the Reformer's heart, it's "This could be better." Your eyes are constantly scanning the environment, identifying areas for improvement. This applies to everything from how a meeting is conducted to the injustices you see plaguing society. At the root of this keen perception lies your core motivation: the desire to live in a world that operates according to the highest standards of goodness, integrity, and justice.

The Desire for Rightness

Reformers possess a profound sense of right and wrong. This doesn't simply mean adhering to conventional rules, but rather, a deeply held belief in principles that transcend rules and regulations. These principles are your guiding light, shaping your decisions, behaviors, and how you view the world. Your internal compass always points towards what you believe should be, fueled by the longing for everything to align with your ideal vision.

This strong sense of rightness makes you a natural advocate for causes you believe in. You see the potential for betterment in every aspect of life, whether it's reforming corrupt systems, making your home more efficient, or elevating the standards of your workplace.

The Drive for Perfection

While your desire for rightness stems from noble intentions, it can sometimes manifest as an underlying drive for perfection. This perfectionism isn't just about achieving flawless results; it's about aligning reality with your deeply ingrained vision of how things ought to be. The frustration arises when the world stubbornly refuses to conform to your ideals.

This perfectionist tendency can sometimes make you critical, both of yourself and others. Remember, while striving for excellence is admirable, the pursuit of absolute perfection is a losing battle and can lead to unnecessary self-pressure and disappointment.

The Benefits of High Standards

Your steadfast commitment to high standards is one of your greatest strengths. This is what makes you a person of integrity, someone who walks the talk and lives by your principles. You are reliable, responsible, and a role model for others. People see your dedication to doing what's right, even if it's unpopular or inconvenient, and it commands respect.

Your eye for detail and high expectations for quality mean that work done by a Reformer is often done exceptionally well. It's less about outward praise and more about the profound inner satisfaction of knowing you've done something to the best of your ability, in alignment with your values.

From Rigidity to Reasonableness

Understanding your core motivation is crucial for growth as a Reformer. It's important to recognize that the world is inherently messy, humans are fallible, and expecting everything to match your ideals is a recipe for frustration. The challenge for Reformers lies in finding a balance between their high standards and accepting the imperfections of reality.

This acceptance doesn't mean resignation. Rather, it's about choosing your battles wisely and focusing your energy on areas where you can make a real, positive impact. It's about applying your Reformer drive with both passion and pragmatism.

Action Steps: Understanding Your Core Motivation

1. **Reflect on Your Ideals:** What are the unwavering principles you hold dear? What values are non-negotiable to you?

2. **Identify Triggers:** What situations make you feel the strongest need to make things right or perfect? How does this manifest in your behavior?

3. **Practice Acceptance:** Find small ways to accept imperfections and acknowledge that sometimes "good enough" really is good enough.

By understanding your core desire for goodness and order, you can harness this power and direct it towards creating meaningful change without letting perfectionism hold you back.

THE IDEALIST'S TOOLKIT: THE HEAD CENTER AND THE REFORMER'S DRIVE FOR CLARITY

The Enneagram system maps out three core centers of intelligence: Head, Heart, and Body. While all three centers are present in everyone, one tends to be dominant for each personality type. For Reformers, the Head Center is where much of your power and perspective reside.

The Thinking Center

The Head Center is associated with intellect, analysis, and logic. It's the realm of thoughts, ideas, and rational decision-making. As a Head Center type, this is where you feel most grounded and secure. You have a natural tendency to think things through carefully, weigh possibilities, and analyze information before taking action.

Your mind is like a powerful processor, constantly filtering, sorting, and making sense of the world around you. This analytical ability gives you an impressive capacity to see both the big picture and the finer details. It allows you to create systems, develop strategies, and identify inconsistencies in a way that's efficient and logical.

Seeking Clarity Above All

The Head Center manifests in Reformers as a deep-seated drive for clarity, order, and understanding. You don't just want things to be 'right,' you want to know exactly *why* they are right, the principles behind them. Ambiguity can be unsettling for you, leading to a persistent search for answers and meaning. This is why Reformers are often drawn to subjects like philosophy, ethics, or areas with well-defined rules and systems.

This love of clarity and structure can make you an excellent problem-solver. You have a knack for untangling complex issues and finding practical solutions. Your ability to reason through situations with a cool head is invaluable, especially in moments of confusion or heightened emotion.

Potential Pitfalls of the Head Center

Your reliance on the Head Center is a tremendous strength, but like any strength, overusing it can create challenges. Here are some potential pitfalls to be mindful of:

- **Overthinking:** Reformers can get caught in analysis paralysis, endlessly weighing options and seeking more information before taking action. Sometimes, you need to trust your intuition and make a move.

- **Rigidity:** Your strong convictions and adherence to logic can sometimes make you appear inflexible or uncompromising, especially when dealing with people who operate more from the Heart Center.

- **Emotional Disconnect:** It's easy to get so focused on rational thought that you lose touch with your feelings, your own or those of others. Remember, empathy and emotional understanding are just as important as intellectual analysis.

Cultivating Balance

As a Reformer, your Head Center is a powerful asset. However, it's essential to balance your intellect with the wisdom of your Heart and Body Centers:

- **Heart Center:** Connect with your compassion, learn to soften your judgments, and allow yourself to simply feel without always analyzing.

- **Body Center:** Tune into your instincts and physical sensations. Getting grounded in your body through exercise, nature, or mindfulness can help quiet a busy mind.

Action Steps: Cultivating Head Center Awareness

1. **Notice Your Analysis:** When do you find yourself over-analyzing or seeking endless information?

2. **Check Your Assumptions:** Your mind is great at creating narratives. Remember, interpretations are not always facts. Challenge your assumptions and consider alternative perspectives.

3. **Get into Your Body:** Engage in physical activities that quiet your mind and allow you to focus on the present moment.

The Reformer's Head Center is a gift, but true balance comes from learning to skillfully integrate all three centers of intelligence. When you embrace the wisdom of your mind, heart, and body, you unlock your full potential as a powerful force for positive change.

THE QUEST FOR IMPROVEMENT: THE REFORMER'S RELATIONSHIP WITH ANGER

Anger, that fiery and often misunderstood emotion, is an inevitable part of the human experience. For Reformers, however, the relationship with anger can be particularly complex. Your strong sense of right and wrong, coupled with the deep desire for improvement, can make you acutely sensitive to actions and behaviors that deviate from your ideals. This sensitivity often triggers a ripple effect, with frustration subtly morphing into a powerful undercurrent of anger.

The Mask of Resentment

While other Enneagram types might express their anger outwardly in visible outbursts, Reformers are more likely to internalize it. This suppressed anger can manifest as resentment, passive-aggression, or the silent withdrawal of approval. You may find yourself biting your tongue to avoid causing conflict, but the anger remains simmering beneath the surface.

The reason for this suppression stems partly from your self-image. Reformers strive to be morally upright, the people who always do the right thing. Outward displays of anger feel contradictory to this image and may even create a sense of inner shame.

The Root of Reformer Anger

Often, a Reformer's anger stems from a perceived violation of their deeply held values. When actions don't match intentions, when someone behaves carelessly or unethically, or when the world operates in ways that seem unfair, the flames of frustration are ignited.

Your anger can also be rooted in the gap between your ideals and the messy realities of life. This disappointment isn't necessarily directed at any one person, but at the imperfections of the world itself. As an idealist, it's incredibly frustrating when things don't go according to your vision of how they *should* be.

The Power (and Potential Pitfalls) of Anger

Anger, like any emotion, is neither good nor bad in itself. It's what we do with it that matters. When channeled consciously, the energy of anger can become a powerful fuel for positive change. It can propel you to speak out against injustice, set healthy boundaries, or push back against complacency.

However, when anger is suppressed or mismanaged, it can become destructive. Unprocessed anger can fester, creating resentment that poisons relationships and chips away at your own inner peace. In extreme cases, it can even manifest as self-righteous judgment, where you start seeing yourself as morally superior to others.

The Path to Healthy Anger Expression

Learning to acknowledge and understand your anger is a crucial step towards growth as a Reformer:

- **Name it:** Don't shy away from the emotion. Allow yourself the space to simply feel angry, without judgment. Recognizing it is the first step towards managing it.

- **Get Curious:** Explore the root of your anger. What value is being violated? What ideal is not being lived up to?

- **Choose Your Outlet:** Find healthy ways to express and release anger – physical exercise, journaling, or honest conversations where you set boundaries assertively but respectfully.

Moving from Resentment to Resolution

Holding onto resentment is like drinking poison and expecting the other person to get sick. Letting go isn't about condoning behavior; it's about releasing the burden you carry. Remember, you can't control others, but you can control your reaction. Sometimes the most powerful action is to communicate clearly and then choose to let it go.

Action Steps: Working with Anger

1. **Body Awareness:** Notice where you feel anger in your body. Do you feel heat rising, muscles tightening? Observing these sensations helps break the cycle of suppression.

2. **Speak Up Kindly:** Don't wait until anger boils over. Practice expressing concerns without letting frustration take the wheel.

3. **Perspective Shift:** Ask yourself, "Will this matter in six months, a year, or five years?" This brings perspective and helps you let go of anger over minor issues.

Anger is a natural human emotion. Learning to harness the Reformer's fiery energy consciously means transforming frustration into a powerful catalyst for change, both within yourself and in the world around you.

BUILDING BRIDGES, NOT WALLS: THE REFORMER'S WINGS AND HOW THEY INFLUENCE BEHAVIOR

Within the Enneagram system, wings are the personality types adjacent to your core type. These wings act like supporting characters, subtly influencing your traits, behaviors, and how you navigate the world. For Reformers, who are Enneagram Type Ones, the possible wings are Type Nine (The Peacemaker) and Type Seven (The Enthusiast).

Understanding Your Dominant Wing

While both wings can play a role in your personality, one typically holds more influence. Your dominant wing adds a unique flavor or nuance to your core Reformer traits. Identifying your dominant wing can bring invaluable insights into your motivations, strengths, and potential blind spots.

Here's a brief overview of how each wing can manifest within the Reformer:

The Reformer with a Nine Wing (1w9)

- **The Idealistic Realist:** This wing brings a touch of the Nine's peace-seeking and accommodating nature to the Reformer's personality. You have a slightly softer edge, with a desire to maintain harmony alongside your drive to make things better.
- **Strengths:** 1w9s are often highly principled while also being diplomatic in their approach to reform. They can see multiple sides of an issue and are more likely to compromise without abandoning their core values.

- **Challenges:** The Nine's tendency towards avoiding conflict can sometimes lead the 1w9 to hesitate too long in speaking up, or they may find themselves suppressing their own needs to maintain peace.

The Reformer with a Seven Wing (1w7)

- **The Enthusiastic Reformer:** The Seven wing injects a dose of optimism and playfulness into the Reformer's typically serious nature. This creates a sense of lightness and a greater openness to new ideas and experiences.
- **Strengths:** 1w7s bring enthusiasm and a can-do attitude to their reform efforts. They are less likely to become bogged down in overthinking and are more inclined to take action and find joy in the process of making improvements.
- **Challenges:** The Seven's impulsiveness and aversion to routine can create inner tension for the 1w7. They may struggle with staying focused on one particular cause or may become scattered in their efforts to fix everything at once.

Uncovering Your Wing

Here are some ways to determine your dominant wing:

- **Online Tests:** Many resources are available online that provide Enneagram tests with wing analysis. Remember, even the best tests are just a starting point for self-exploration.
- **Inner Reflection:** Consider the characteristics outlined above. Which wing description resonates most with your experience? When do you feel the inner tension between your Reformer core and the pull of one of the wings?
- **Observe Yourself:** Pay attention to your behaviors when stressed or relaxed. Your wing may become more pronounced in these situations.

Embracing Your Wing

Your wing is an integral part of your personality, offering both gifts and potential growth areas:

- **Harness the Strengths:** Identify the talents and positive traits associated with your wing and consciously lean into them.
- **Mitigate the Challenges:** Be mindful of the potential pitfalls of your wing and work toward cultivating balance. If you're a 1w9, practice speaking up for yourself. If you're a 1w7, develop discipline and follow-through.
- **Integrate:** Your wing isn't meant to override your Reformer nature but rather add nuance and dimension to it. Find ways to express both your Reformer core and your wing in a balanced and harmonious way.

Action Steps: Exploring Your Wing

1. **Wing Test:** Take an Enneagram test that analyzes your dominant wing. Reflect on the accuracy of the results.
2. **Triggers and Gifts:** What situations make you feel the traits of your wing most strongly? Observe the benefits and challenges you experience.
3. **Seek Feedback:** Ask trusted friends or loved ones if they recognize aspects of either the Seven or Nine in your personality.

By understanding the unique flavor your wing brings to your Reformer personality, you gain a deeper level of self-awareness. Embrace this additional dimension of yourself, allowing it to enrich your journey of growth and your capacity to create positive change in the world.

THE REFORMER AS EIGHT: EMBRACING ASSERTIVENESS FOR POSITIVE CHANGE

While your core personality type is the Reformer, your wings are not the only source of influence within the Enneagram system. One key concept is the idea of "stress" and "security" lines. These lines connect your core type to two other Enneagram types, revealing how your behavior and motivations might shift under different circumstances.

For Reformers, the "security" connection is to Type Four (The Individualist), bringing in a touch of sensitivity and introspection. However, it's the "stress" connection to Type Eight (The Challenger) that we'll delve into in this chapter.

When "The Reformer" Wears the Cloak of "The Challenger"

Under conditions of stress or when your core Reformer drive for justice feels threatened, you may unconsciously take on some of the qualities of the Eight. This isn't about suddenly becoming a different personality type but rather, tapping into a different set of resources available within your inner landscape.

Here's how the traits of the Eight tend to manifest in a stressed Reformer:

- **Strength and Assertiveness:** Eights are known for their boldness, directness, and ability to take charge. When in "Eight mode," you become less concerned about diplomacy and more focused on asserting your ideals with unwavering confidence and strength.
- **Confrontation:** Eights don't shy away from conflict when something important is at stake. Under stress, your typical desire for harmony might give way to a willingness

to confront situations or people head-on, powered by a protective energy.

- **Decisiveness:** The Eight's "take charge" energy can help a Reformer break free from overthinking and analysis paralysis. In this mode, you become more decisive and less hindered by self-doubt.
- **Intensity:** A sense of urgency and fierce intensity can infuse your approach, pushing back against anything that threatens your ideals or attempts to impede necessary reforms.

The Potential Pitfalls of Over-Reliance on Eight Energy

While the Eight's energy can be a powerful tool for Reformers in certain situations, relying on it too heavily can lead to imbalances:

- **Aggression:** Sometimes, healthy assertiveness can tip into outright aggression, especially if the Reformer's righteous anger becomes unchecked.
- **Control:** In an attempt to ensure things are done their way, Reformers in "Eight mode" can become controlling or domineering, alienating those they wish to influence.
- **Lack of Empathy:** The Eight's focus on strength and action can sometimes lead to overlooking the feelings and perspectives of others.
- **Impatience:** Reformers, who are already prone to frustration, may become incredibly impatient when channeling this fiery Eight energy.

Harnessing Eight Power Consciously

The key is to utilize the positive aspects of the Eight's energy intentionally, not letting stress control your response:

- **Channel Anger Productively:** Instead of suppressing anger as you might typically do, channel it into action that creates change.
- **Speak Truth to Power:** When necessary, draw on your inner Eight to confront systems, individuals, or beliefs that violate

your principles.

- **Protect the Vulnerable:** Find your Eight-like fierceness to defend those who are treated unjustly or who are unable to stand up for themselves.
- **Take Leadership:** Step into Eight-like leadership roles when progress stalls and decisive action is needed to make things happen.

Action Steps: Embracing Healthy Eight Energy

1. **Notice Your Shifts:** Observe those moments where you feel the internal shift towards a more assertive, Eight-like approach. What triggers this change?
2. **Use Physical Outlets:** Find healthy ways to embody the Eight's strength – engage in intense workouts or forms of movement that allow you to express power physically.
3. **Set Clear Boundaries:** Practice saying 'no' firmly when needed and setting boundaries to protect your time and energy. Notice how this feels different from your usual approach.

Remember, channeling Eight energy is about accessing your inner reserves of strength and boldness to enact positive change. By consciously harnessing this power, you magnify your capacity to make a real difference in the world.

THE REFORMER AS SEVEN: BALANCING VISION WITH PRAGMATISM

In the dynamic world of the Enneagram, your connection to Type Seven (The Enthusiast), offers the potential to inject a much-needed dose of lightness, playfulness, and adaptability into the Reformer's focused and principled nature. While this influence may not be as immediately prominent as the connection to Type Eight, the Seven holds valuable gifts for Reformers willing to explore a broader perspective.

The Influence of the Seven

Here's how the Seven's energy can subtly (or sometimes not so subtly) manifest in Reformers:

- **Openness to Possibility:** Sevens are natural optimists always seeking new experiences and possibilities. This influence can help Reformers break out of rigid thinking and consider alternative approaches to improvement and problem-solving.
- **Increased Spontaneity:** The Seven's spontaneous nature can soften the Reformer's tendency toward strict adherence to plans and routines. Channeling this energy invites moments of joy and a lightness of spirit into your life.
- **Flexibility:** Sevens excel at adapting and finding creative solutions in difficult situations. This adaptability can help Reformers navigate unexpected setbacks or roadblocks toward their goals, encouraging greater resilience.
- **Perspective Shift:** Reformers tend to focus intensely on what's wrong, while Sevens see the fun and potential in every situation. Shifting towards this Seven-influenced

perspective helps balance your inherent intensity and reveals a brighter, more playful side of life.

Potential Challenges

Like any borrowed energy, there's always the potential for over-reliance or imbalance:

- **Flakiness:** While the Seven's adventurous spirit is refreshing for Reformers, too much of it can lead to impulsiveness, scattered focus, or an inability to follow through on projects.
- **Avoidance of Difficult Emotions:** Sevens are experts at seeking pleasure and avoiding pain. For Reformers, this influence could lead to temporarily glossing over uncomfortable feelings or truths in favor of distraction.
- **Fear of Boredom:** Sevens dislike routine. This influence, left unchecked, can push Reformers to jump from one "perfecting" project to another, failing to find satisfaction in steady progress or the completion of a task.
- **Reduced Self-Discipline:** Sevens focus on what feels good in the moment. Leaning too heavily on this energy can erode the Reformer's strong sense of self-discipline, leading to procrastination or indulging in distractions.

Integrating Seven Energy for Growth

Here's how to cultivate a healthy relationship with your inner seven:

- **Embrace the Joy of Learning:** Approach the task of improvement with the curiosity and wonder of a Seven seeking out a new adventure.
- **Plan for Spontaneity:** Channel the Seven's playfulness by building flexibility into your schedule. Allow space for unplanned experiences, even if it's just a few hours each week.
- **Reframe Negatives:** Notice your tendency to focus on what needs fixing. Practice the Seven's approach of consciously seeking out the positive aspects of a situation, person, or

even yourself.

- **The Power of Play:** Engage in activities that are purely for fun and enjoyment – things that have no purpose other than sparking joy and bringing a sense of lightness to your heart.

Action Steps: Embracing Healthy Seven Energy

1. **Fun List:** Create a list of activities that feel purely fun and energizing. Make a commitment to incorporate one of these items into your life each week.
2. **Seek Novelty:** Break your usual routine! try a new restaurant, explore a different neighborhood, or learn a new hobby just for the joy of it.
3. **Gratitude Glasses:** Practice the Seven's perspective by finding at least three things to be grateful for each day, no matter how small they may seem.

The Reformer archetype often comes with seriousness and intensity. Embracing the playfulness and optimism of the Seven injects some much-needed sunshine into your perspective. Blending discipline with pleasure, and vision with pragmatism, ultimately helps you live a richer, more balanced life while leaving your uniquely positive mark on the world.

THE POWER OF PRINCIPLES: ETHICS AND THE REFORMER'S DECISION-MAKING

One of the defining characteristics of the Reformer personality is your deeply ingrained sense of right and wrong. You hold yourself to exceptionally high standards and possess a strong moral compass that shapes your thoughts, actions, and how you navigate the nuances of the world. This unwavering commitment to ethics can be both your greatest strength and, at times, a potential challenge.

The Principled Reformer

Let's explore the qualities that make Reformers so naturally principled:

- **Clear Value System:** You have a well-defined set of ideals and beliefs that guide your decision-making. These principles are like beacons, illuminating the path of what you deem to be the "right" way to conduct yourself and the "right" way to shape the world.
- **Integrity:** Reformers walk the talk. You don't simply hold high standards for yourself; you feel a deep responsibility to live according to those standards, even when it's inconvenient or difficult.
- **Sense of Mission:** Your commitment to improvement isn't just about yourself. You have a sense of duty to do your part to make the world a more just and ethical place, often taking advocacy roles or positions where you can lead by example.

The Challenge of the Gray Areas

In an ideal world, the lines between right and wrong would always be crystal clear. Unfortunately, life is rarely that black and white.

As a Reformer, your tendency to see the world in these terms can create inner conflict and frustration when faced with complex situations or moral dilemmas. This is where the challenge of navigating the gray areas arises.

Here are some potential difficulties Reformers might face due to their rigid adherence to principles:

- **Inflexibility:** A strong moral compass is a powerful tool, but it can also lead to a judgmental attitude or an inability to see alternative perspectives when the situation calls for flexibility.
- **Missed Opportunities:** Overly rigid thinking can make you dismiss options or compromises that, while not perfectly aligned with your ideals, could still bring about positive change in an imperfect world.
- **Black and White Thinking:** The desire to see the world neatly categorized into good and bad can make forgiving transgressions or extending grace to others a challenge, even if their intentions were well-meaning.

Cultivating Moral Flexibility

Striving for improvement and upholding your ethical standards should be a source of strength, not a cause for constant inner turmoil. It's essential to soften your approach in certain situations:

- **Challenge Assumptions:** Remember, your interpretation of what is "right" is just that – an interpretation. Seek out differing viewpoints and be willing to consider if your perspective is too rigid.
- **Zoom Out:** Step back from the details of a situation to assess the bigger picture. Does upholding one particular principle outweigh potential benefits of a compromise that still advances some form of positive change?
- **Empathy as a Guide:** Your Head Center is dominant, but don't neglect your Heart Center. Connect with compassion

for yourself and for others who might be operating from a different set of principles or experiences.

Action Steps: Navigating Ethical Dilemmas

1. **Define Your Non-Negotiables:** Identify the core values that are unwavering for you. These act as your ethical foundation.
2. **Identify the Gray:** In what areas of life do you struggle most with compromise or ambiguity? Target these areas for growth.
3. **Seek Counsel:** Discuss ethical complexities with someone you trust who may offer alternative perspectives and help you see shades of gray you might have missed.

It's important to remember that having strong principles doesn't mean being inflexible. True moral development lies in finding a balance between uncompromising adherence to your core values and the ability to skillfully navigate those complex situations where the "right" choice isn't always clear.

FRIENDSHIP AND THE REFORMER: BUILDING STRONG CONNECTIONS THROUGH SHARED VALUES

As a Reformer, your desire for meaning and your focus on improving the world might lead you to underestimate the importance of friendship and interpersonal connection. While you deeply value loyalty and righteousness, forming and maintaining close friendships can sometimes feel challenging, especially if those bonds don't align with your strong sense of purpose.

Potential Friendship Challenges for Reformers

Let's take a closer look at some of the factors that can make cultivating friendships a bit less intuitive for Reformers:

- **High Expectations:** Reformers tend to apply their high standards to friendships as well. You may find yourself easily disappointed when friends don't measure up to your ideals of how a "good" friend should behave.
- **Critical Tendencies:** Your strong inner critic can spill into your interactions with others, leading you to focus on flaws or behaviors in your friends that you deem in need of "improvement."
- **Lack of Time & Energy:** With a full plate of work, reforms to enact, and ideals to uphold, dedicating time and emotional energy to building friendships may not always feel like a high priority.
- **"All or Nothing" Mentality:** Reformers tend to value depth over breadth. You may struggle with more casual friendships, seeking out those rare souls who fully align with

your values and perspective.

Why Friendship Matters

Despite these challenges, friendships are a vital aspect of life for Reformers, offering benefits like:

- **Joy and Relaxation:** Close friendships offer a safe space to let down your guard, experience laughter, and simply enjoy the present moment without the weight of self-improvement.
- **Support System:** True friends provide emotional support during hard times, a listening ear when you need to vent, and genuine celebration of your achievements.
- **Personal Growth:** Good friends challenge you, expose you to different viewpoints, and gently hold a mirror up to your blindspots, all essential aspects of growth.
- **Connection and Belonging:** Deep friendships provide a sense of belonging and connection, a reminder that you're not alone in your quest for a better world.

The Kind of Friends a Reformer Needs

Reformers thrive with friends who have these qualities:

- **Integrity:** Friends who share your core values and ethical standards are essential. These friendships provide a bedrock of trust and mutual respect.
- **Intellectual Curiosity:** Seek out friends who are as passionate about ideas as you are, those who engage in thought-provoking conversations and challenge your perspective.
- **Patience and Understanding:** True friends accept your quirks, your perfectionist tendencies, and your occasional critical voice. They offer unconditional support and a safe space for you to be your imperfect self.
- **A Sense of Fun:** Friends who help you let loose, tap into your playful side, and remind you that life is to be enjoyed as well as improved are precious gifts.

Action Steps: Cultivating Meaningful Friendship

1. **Shift Your Focus:** Instead of focusing on a potential friend's flaws, actively look for their positive qualities and what they can teach YOU.
2. **Let Go of Perfection:** Accept that your friends won't be carbon copies of yourself. Appreciate their unique perspectives and strengths.
3. **Be Vulnerable:** Sharing imperfections and needs fosters deeper connection. True friends will welcome the real you without judgment.
4. **Invest Time:** Make a conscious effort to schedule regular catch-ups, phone calls, or shared activities. Friendship takes nurturing.

Building deep and lasting friendships as a Reformer requires a conscious effort to step outside your comfort zone. Yet, the rewards are immense. Seek out those who support your mission, encourage your growth, and remind you that a life well-lived includes both the pursuit of improvement and the simple joys of genuine connection.

THE REFORMER IN LOVE: SEEKING A PARTNER WHO SHARES THE VISION

Just as you approach all things in life with intention and high ideals, so too does love fall under the scrutiny of the Reformer. You don't settle in any aspect of your existence, and seeking a romantic partner is no exception. As a person driven by a deep desire for integrity and improvement, love holds a special meaning, a chance to build a life with someone who shares your journey and fuels your passion for making the world a better place.

The Reformer's Ideal Partner

When Reformers envision their ideal partner, the focus isn't solely on romantic chemistry or shared interests, although those are important. Your heart yearns for a partner who embodies:

- **Shared Values:** More than anything else, your ideal partner must hold core values that align with your own. These shared principles create a foundation of trust and an unshakable belief in your shared goals for a more just and equitable world.

- **Intellectual Stimulation:** A partner who sparks lively debates, brings in new perspectives, and pushes you to think more deeply about important issues is incredibly attractive to the Reformer mind.

- **Strong Moral Compass:** You want a partner who takes ethics and responsibility as seriously as you do. Someone with a strong sense of integrity and a commitment to doing what's right strengthens your sense of being a team.

- **Mutual Growth:** You seek a partner who is equally invested in self-improvement and personal growth. A relationship that encourages both partners to become better versions of themselves is the ultimate ideal.

Challenges in Love as a Reformer

Finding a partner who embodies all these qualities can feel like a daunting task, and your Reformer nature may present some hurdles to navigate along the way:

- **Unrealistic Expectations:** While having high standards is a strength, expecting absolute perfection in a partner creates unrealistic expectations and a potential for constant disappointment.
- **Controlling Tendencies:** Your drive to improve things can sometimes translate to trying to improve your partner. This controlling tendency can create resentment and a lack of acceptance for who they are as an individual.
- **Emotional Openness:** While Reformers feel deeply, expressing emotions doesn't always come easily. Vulnerability can be challenging, but it's vital for creating a deep connection and feeling safe in a relationship.
- **Work-Life Balance:** Your commitment to your mission can lead to prioritizing work over romantic relationships, unintentionally placing them on the back burner.

Cultivating Healthy Love as a Reformer

Embracing love as a Reformer requires a conscious effort to soften certain tendencies while still seeking a partner who enhances your life and mission:

- **Acceptance Over Perfection:** Accept flaws, both in others and in yourself. Perfect humans don't exist, but partners who perfectly share your vision and enhance your life do.
- **Communication Over Criticism:** When you feel the urge to 'correct' something, practice expressing your needs clearly and respectfully without judgment.
- **Embrace Vulnerability:** Remember that letting your

guard down and expressing emotions is a sign of strength, not weakness. True intimacy comes through shared vulnerability.

- **Carve Out Time for Love:** Just as you dedicate time to other aspects of self-improvement, consciously make space for love and connection, allowing it to nurture other areas of your life.

Action Steps: Finding the Right Partner

1. **Beyond the Checklist:** Write out your non-negotiable values and qualities, but also allow yourself to be surprised by those who don't tick every box but bring unexpected joy.
2. **Focus on Shared Purpose:** Seek out potential partners in environments aligned with your ideals - volunteer work, advocacy groups, or causes you care about.
3. **Be the Partner You Seek** Embody the qualities you'd hope to find in a partner – integrity, commitment to growth, emotional honesty. Like attracts like.

The Reformer's approach to love may be unconventional, but it's guided by a profound desire for a partnership rooted in deep meaning and a shared mission for good. With awareness of your potential pitfalls and a willingness to soften your edges, you'll find a love that not only fills your heart but also fuels your passion to leave the world a better place than you found it.

THE REFORMER AT WORK: LEADING WITH INTEGRITY AND INSPIRING OTHERS

The workplace is an environment ripe for a Reformer's talents. Armed with a strong work ethic, a dedication to quality standards, and a desire to improve systems and processes, you excel in roles that allow you to make a meaningful impact. However, certain aspects of standard work environments might clash with your idealistic nature, creating challenges if not approached with awareness.

The Strengths of a Reformer at Work

Let's delve into the qualities that make Reformers natural assets to any team:

- **Mission-Driven:** You are a natural advocate for causes you believe in, and this translates powerfully to the workplace. Reformers don't just punch a clock; they bring a sense of mission and higher purpose to their work.
- **Systems Thinker:** With your ability to see the big picture and identify inefficiencies, you're adept at finding innovative solutions to existing problems and streamlining processes for improvement.
- **Unyielding Standards:** You refuse to settle for mediocrity. Your commitment to excellence elevates the quality of work for both yourself and those around you.
- **Reliability:** Reformers can be counted on to deliver on time, to high standards. You take your responsibilities incredibly seriously and won't rest until the task is done correctly.
- **Natural Leader:** With your integrity, strong work ethic, and dedication to a shared vision, you become a leader others

want to follow, whether you have a formal leadership role or not.

Potential Work Challenges for Reformers

Of course, every strength, when overused, becomes a weakness. Here are some challenges Reformers need to be mindful of in the workplace:

- **Impatience with Inefficiency:** Seeing sub-par work, outdated methods, or a lack of commitment to a worthy mission fuels your inner fire. However, this can lead to frustration and criticism directed at colleagues.
- **Unrealistic Expectations:** Your high standards can sometimes push you to expect too much from yourself and your coworkers, creating an atmosphere of dissatisfaction or burnout.
- **Workaholic Tendencies:** Your dedication can lead to blurring the lines between work time and personal time. It's important to set healthy boundaries to ensure you're not sacrificing your well-being.
- **Difficulty Delegating:** The desire to see things done 'correctly' can make it hard to entrust tasks to others. This can become a roadblock to your own advancement and can create resentment among teammates.

Embracing Leadership as a Reformer

Reformers make for impactful leaders due to their:

- **Clear Vision:** You inspire others with your well-articulated vision and your unwavering belief in a better way of doing things.
- **Ethical Approach:** You gain respect by making decisions grounded in sound principles and a commitment to fairness for all involved.
- **Empowering Style:** While you have high expectations, you also empower your team, providing them with the tools and support to develop and excel.

Action Steps: Thriving in the Workplace

1. **Temper Your Intensity:** Channel your frustration with inefficiency into finding productive solutions. Focus on what you can control and influence.
2. **Practice Acceptance:** Not everyone shares your ideals. Find a balance between pushing for excellence and accepting that your colleagues won't always match your passion.
3. **Praise Effort:** Notice and acknowledge hard work and good intentions in others, even if the result isn't perfect. This builds trust and camaraderie.
4. **Delegate Strategically:** Start small. Give team members tasks commensurate with their skill levels and offer mentorship to help them progress.

The Reformer's natural drive and ethical approach make you a powerful force for good in any workplace. Find roles that leverage your talents, embrace positions of leadership, and remember that sometimes the most significant impact comes from inspiring others to strive for excellence, not by doing it all yourself.

THE SHADOW SIDE: WHEN REFORM TURNS INTO CRITICISM

Like all personality types, Reformers have a shadow side. This refers to a collection of suppressed traits or tendencies that emerge under pressure or when your core strengths become overused. Understanding your shadow side is crucial for personal growth, as it sheds light on behaviors that might sabotage your well-being, relationships, and your overall capacity for positive impact.

The Critical Reformer

The shadow side of the Reformer manifests most prominently as excessive criticism – of others, of yourself, and sometimes even of situations the Reformer has no control over. Here's how it can show up:

- **The Harsh Judge:** The inner critic, always on alert, becomes amplified. You relentlessly focus on flaws, failing to see the big picture or acknowledging the positive aspects of situations or individuals.
- **Outward Criticism:** This inner judgment extends outwards. Friends, colleagues, and loved ones feel the sting of your critical remarks. What's intended as constructive feedback can become demoralizing due to its constant and sometimes harsh nature.
- **Nitpicking and Perfectionism:** Your need for order and perfection kicks into overdrive. You fixate on minor details and lose sight of the ultimate goal, making it difficult to find satisfaction in any achievement, your own or others.
- **Moral Superiority:** When deeply in the grip of their shadow side, Reformers might start viewing themselves as morally "better" than others. This righteous judgmentalism pushes

people away and erodes the Reformer's own joy.

- **Unyielding Rigidity:** Your adherence to your own ideals becomes inflexible. Any deviation from what you deem "right" feels like a personal affront, leading to a loss of compassion and a shutting down of open dialogue.

The Root of the Shadow Side

At its core, this critical shadow side stems from a combination of factors:

- **Unresolved Anger:** Suppressed anger that lacks healthy outlets often transforms into a critical attitude and harsh judgment.
- **Fear of Failure:** The relentless pursuit of perfection can be fueled by a deep fear of not being good enough, of failing to live up to your impossibly high standards.
- **Desire for Control:** Criticism becomes a way of trying to control external factors to maintain an illusion of order and 'rightness' in a world that often feels chaotic.

The Cost of Criticism

Left unchecked, the shadow side of criticism has serious consequences:

- **Strained Relationships:** Constant criticism, even well-intentioned, erodes trust and creates emotional distance.
- **Alienating Others:** People might avoid sharing ideas or seeking collaboration, fearing they'll be met with judgment rather than support.
- **Loss of Perspective:** When fixated on the negative, you miss the bigger picture, the good in people and situations, and you stifle creative problem-solving.
- **Burnout:** Living in a constant state of judgment and dissatisfaction leads to both mental and physical burnout.

Finding Freedom from the Shadow Side

Here's how you can start to find balance and minimize the impact of your shadow side:

- **Notice Your Critic:** Become an observer of your own mind. Recognize when the inner critic starts its relentless tirade and challenge its assumptions.
- **Practice Gratitude:** Shift focus intentionally. Actively seek out things to be grateful for, no matter how small, to counter your natural tendency to fixate on flaws.
- **Choose Your Battles:** Ask yourself, "Will this matter a year from now?" Learn to let go of the small stuff and conserve your energy for what truly matters.
- **Focus on Progress Not Perfection:** Celebrate incremental progress in others and, importantly, in yourself. Recognize that growth takes time.
- **Nurture Your Heart Center:** Activities that connect you to your emotions are essential – journaling, creative expression, time in nature. soften the iron grip of the Head Center.

Action Steps: Taming Your Inner Critic

1. **The Praise Jar:** For every critical thought, write down something positive you notice about yourself or others. Add it to the jar and reflect on it weekly.
2. **Challenge Your Assumptions:** When you find yourself fixating on flaws, ask, "Is there another perspective? What positive qualities might I be overlooking?"
3. **"Good Enough" Practice:** Intentionally choose one small task each day and do it to 'good enough' standards even if it makes you uncomfortable.

Taming your shadow side isn't about eliminating your critical voice altogether; it's about harnessing it for good. With conscious effort, you'll transform your critical energy into a catalyst for positive change, all while preserving your inner peace and creating stronger connections with those around you.

FROM FRUSTRATION TO FULFILLMENT: GROWTH OPPORTUNITIES FOR THE REFORMER

As a Reformer, you're no stranger to the feeling of frustration that often accompanies your unwavering desire to create a more just and perfect world. This frustration stems from the gap between your ideals and the messy realities you encounter, and from the inner tug-of-war between your high standards and your compassionate heart. Yet, within this struggle lies the potential for immense growth and the key to unlocking true fulfillment.

Embracing Frustration as a Catalyst

Instead of viewing frustration as a negative, consider it a powerful motivating force. Here's how healthy frustration can drive you forward:

- **Propels Action:** When confronted with injustice or situations at odds with your ideals, that surge of frustration can be the catalyst for positive change. It pushes you to speak out, take action, or rally others to your cause.
- **Reveals Your Values:** Moments of heightened frustration often illuminate your most cherished values. That anger and disappointment you feel signal what truly matters to you, guiding your focus and energy.
- **Fuels Creativity:** The tension between what is and what could be can spark innovative solutions. Channel your frustration into creative problem-solving and visionary reform strategies.

Growth Opportunities: Where Frustration Meets Potential

Here are key areas where you can turn moments of frustration into opportunities for profound development:

1. **Patience and Acceptance:** The world won't change overnight, and others won't always adopt your ideals as quickly as you'd like. Cultivating patience isn't about resignation, but accepting you can't control everything, only your response. Balance your urgency with acceptance of the often slow pace of change.

2. **Flexibility Without Compromise:** Learn to be adaptable and find alternative ways to bring about positive change without abandoning your core principles. Remember, sometimes a small step forward is better than no progress at all.

3. **From Harshness to Compassion:** It's possible to be both principled and compassionate. Channel your frustrated energy into acts of kindness and understanding, even towards those you disagree with. This softens your approach and creates more openness to dialogue and collaboration.

4. **Self-Compassion Over Self-Criticism:** When the world fails to live up to your standards, extend some of that compassion inward. Recognize that you're doing your best in an imperfect world and acknowledge your own efforts. This prevents frustration from morphing into burnout or debilitating self-criticism.

5. **Finding Joy in the Process:** The journey towards a better world holds its own rewards. Learn to find joy in the act of striving, in the camaraderie with fellow reformers, and in the small victories along the way. This will sustain your long-term commitment to reform.

Action Steps: Leaning Into Growth

1. **Identify Your Triggers:** What situations or behaviors consistently ignite your frustration? Understanding your triggers helps you anticipate challenging moments.

2. **Reframe Your Response:** When you feel that surge of frustration, pause. Ask yourself: "How can I channel this energy productively?"

3. **Perspective Shift:** Practice the Seven's lens: Seek out the positive aspect of a frustrating situation or a person's actions. This expands your view and calms agitation.

4. **Cultivate Mindfulness:** Daily mindfulness practice grounds you in the present moment, reducing reactivity and fostering greater acceptance.

The Path to Fulfillment

True fulfillment for Reformers comes not from the world suddenly conforming to your ideals but from embracing the ever-evolving journey of self-improvement and fighting the good fight with a balance of unwavering determination and compassionate understanding. It's about utilizing your incredible strengths, working skillfully with your potential challenges, and never losing sight of the noble vision that drives you forward.

THE REFORMER'S LEGACY: CREATING A MORE JUST AND EQUITABLE WORLD

As a Reformer, your desire to leave the world a better place than you found it runs deep. You possess the unwavering determination, ethical clarity, and visionary leadership to create a tangible, positive impact. This chapter explores how you can harness your innate Reformer strengths to establish a legacy defined by meaningful contribution and lasting reform.

Identifying Your Unique Sphere of Influence

Start by pinpointing where your passions and talents can have the most significant influence. Here's a framework for your reflection:

- **Strengths and Interests:** What are you naturally good at? What topics ignite your passion and motivate you to take informed action?
- **Community Needs:** What problems or injustices do you see in your community or the world? Where does the current system fail to uphold your values?
- **The Power of Intersection:** Find the unique point where your strengths, passions, and the world's needs intersect. This is where your potential for legacy is most powerful.

Strategies for Creating Impact

Once you've clarified your focus, consider these avenues for leveraging your Reformer strengths:

- **Advocacy:** Raise your voice! Speak out against injustices, share your informed insights on platforms that reach a wider audience, and support organizations working towards causes you believe in.

- **Direct Action:** Get involved! Volunteer your time and skills, participate in grassroots movements for change, or use your expertise to create solutions that directly improve the lives of others.
- **Mentorship:** Empower the next generation of reformers. Share your knowledge, experience, and passion to guide and inspire others on their path toward creating positive change.
- **Ethical Leadership:** Step into positions of leadership, whether in your career, family, or community. Influence others by modeling integrity, advocating for fairness, and implementing ethical systems that create long-term good.
- **Systematic Change:** Tackle the root causes of the issues that concern you most. Think big! Work towards policy reform, develop innovative new models, or challenge the status quo to create a more just system for all.

Legacy with a Reformer Touch

Your Reformer nature infuses your mission with these powerful qualities:

- **Vision with Practicality:** Marry your big-picture vision of a better world with the Reformer's knack for creating actionable plans and efficient strategies.
- **Ethical Leadership:** Your strong moral compass ensures that your legacy is not just about the results but about getting there with integrity in every step of the process.
- **Long-Term Impact:** You're not looking for quick fixes. Aim for systemic change, creating reforms that create a sustainable, positive impact for generations to come.

Pitfalls to Avoid

As with any endeavor, there are challenges to navigate:

- **Burnout:** Your passion can sometimes lead to overworking. Pace yourself, find healthy outlets for stress, and prioritize self-care to ensure your legacy work is a marathon and not a sprint.

- **Letting Perfect be the Enemy of the Good:** Focus on progress over perfection. Don't let your pursuit of the ideal stand in the way of achieving meaningful, incremental change.
- **Losing Heart:** Setbacks will occur. Cultivate resilience and remember that even small victories play a role in the larger tapestry of creating a better world.

Action Steps: Building Your Legacy

1. **Refine Your Vision:** Write out your ultimate vision for the future. What would a perfect world look like in terms of the cause you champion?
2. **Break it Down:** Identify concrete steps and goals that move you incrementally closer to that vision. Start with small, achievable actions and build from there.
3. **Seek Collaboration:** Join forces with like-minded individuals and organizations. Pooling resources and talents amplifies the impact of your reform efforts.
4. **Share Your Story:** Inspire others by sharing the challenges and victories along your path to creating a legacy of positive change.

The Reformer's relentless drive for improvement doesn't end with your internal world. Channel that same passion and unwavering belief in a better future to make your mark on the world around you. Let your legacy be one defined by the relentless pursuit of justice, ethical leadership, and a commitment to leaving the world in a better state than you found it.

THE IDEALIST IN ACTION: PUTTING YOUR REFORMER STRENGTHS TO WORK

This final chapter is the culmination of your journey through "The Reformer: The Idealist's Guide to the Real World." It's time to synthesize what you've learned about your Reformer nature and translate your strengths, passions, and growth areas into concrete actions that create a positive ripple effect in the world.

Harnessing Your Strengths for Good

As a reminder, here are some of the core strengths that define the Reformer personality:

- **Ethical Compass:** Your unwavering commitment to principles guides every action you take.
- **Clarity of Vision:** You envision a better world and hold yourself accountable to make it happen.
- **Dedication to Improvement:** Not just for yourself - you seek constant growth and improvement for the systems and communities around you.
- **Leadership Potential:** Your ability to inspire, organize, and advocate makes you a natural change-maker.

Areas for Continued Growth

Let's revisit some common Reformer challenges to be aware of as you step fully into your role as an agent of change:

- **Perfectionism:** Remind yourself that progress matters more than unattainable perfection.
- **Intensity:** At times, soften your delivery to build bridges with those who have different communication styles.
- **Balancing Head and Heart:** Practice empathy and

compassion alongside your dedication to principles.

- **Rest and Recharge:** Passion is powerful, but burnout is harmful. Make self-care a priority.

The Reformer in Different Domains of Life

Here's how you can put your Reformer strengths to work, keeping your potential growth areas in mind, across different areas of your life:

- **At Work:** Become a champion of ethical practices. Design efficient systems for improvement. Mentor and empower colleagues to reach their potential.
- **In Relationships:** Practice compassionate communication. Model integrity and healthy boundaries. Express appreciation and focus on the positives.
- **In Your Community:** Advocate for causes you believe in. Volunteer your time and expertise. Lead or join groups dedicated to positive reform.
- **The Everyday Reformer:** Make conscious choices that align with your values. Support ethical businesses. Educate yourself on important issues.

Action Steps: From Theory to Practice

1. **Revisit Your Values:** Start with a clear articulation of your core values. What matters most to you? What kind of world do you want to be part of creating?

2. **Identify Your Sphere of Influence:** Where can you have the most impact? Consider your community, your workplace, and your personal networks.

3. **Small Steps, Big Impact:** Choose ONE action step, no matter how small, that brings you closer to acting on your values. Do this daily.

4. **Seek Support:** Connect with like-minded reformers.

Having a community enhances motivation and provides opportunities to leverage collective power.

5. **Celebrate Progress:** Focus on consistent action over dramatic results. Recognize and celebrate both your personal growth and the positive changes you help create.

The Power of Choice

As a Reformer, your desire for a better world is a constant. However, it's ultimately up to you to channel your idealism, your frustration, and your passion into purposeful action. Choose to lead with integrity, strive for constant improvement in yourself and the world around you, and inspire others to do the same. Choose to embrace the Reformer's journey, with its challenges and triumphs, knowing that your work makes a difference.

Remember, change starts with you, with this moment, and the next small step. Let your Reformer light shine and help create a world that reflects the very best of what humanity can be.